THE SEASONS

Louis Lawrence

Foreword by Roy Strong

NELSON CANADA LIMITED

Published in Canada in 1981 by
Nelson Canada Limited
1120 Birchmount Road
Scarborough, Ontario
M1K 5G4

First published in Great Britain 1981 by
Webb & Bower (Publishers) Limited,
33 Southernhay East, Exeter, Devon, EX1 1NS

ISBN: 0–17–601540–X (Standard)
ISBN: 0–17–601541–8 (Special)

Printed and bound in Italy by Arnoldo Mondadori Editore

FOREWORD

Roy Strong

The Seasons was compiled between the years 1887 and 1890 by Louis Lawrence, a publicity artist for Maws, the London chemist. He died an old man in 1945 so that what we have is a work of his youth, the efforts of someone in his late teens in the year of Queen Victoria's Golden Jubilee. There is nothing to indicate that it was the product of an artist with any art-school training, but rather of someone who was learning by way of apprenticeship and by copying what he saw around him. And in this lies part of its peculiar charm.

What sort of setting does *The Seasons* spring from and why does it cast a spell? Its milieu is the modest moral world of late Victorian lower middle-class life with its evangelical piety, its cultivation of God expressed in nature, its sentiment for hearth and home and the virtues of family life. It therefore epitomizes for us a lost security romanticized by living memory that can just about reach that far back. The essence of the book is, of course, its texts. Tennyson, Longfellow, Shelley and Scott are quoted, but there are also the "many others" to whom Lawrence refers, totally forgotten purveyors of morally uplifting verse for the family: the Rev. R. Wilton, Mary Eugenia, the Rev. A.A. Graley or H.P. Spofford. The tradition of this type of poetry we catch in its death-throes today in Christmas card verses which continue to reveal the strength of the hold of this formula that interlocked pictured image and virtuous thought in lyric form.

The Seasons is an offspring of that ethos. It belongs to the atmosphere of home life before the advent of the car, radio or television. Family entertainment consisted in reading, making music and hobbies, all of which were edited down once a week to those activities regarded as suitable for the Lord's Day. *The Seasons* is essentially a Sunday book. M.V. Hughes in the first volume of her trilogy entitled *A London Child of the 1870s* recalls that on that day "all amusements, as well as work, were forbidden. It was a real privation not to be allowed to draw and paint. However, an exception was made in favour of illuminated texts . . .". One can visualize *The Seasons* being the result of just such a situation.

It also reflects another late Victorian phenomenon, the holiday, the railways opening up England to classes of society that before had never travelled for leisure. The beauties of nature and the picturesque charm of town and village are what the guidebooks dwell upon. Lawrence obviously frequented the Isle of Wight, first made fashionable by Victoria and Albert. In *The Seasons* the village of Bonchurch, close to Ventnor, figures with its pond, as well as Carisbrook Castle and Shanklin. Hastings and Dover, both easily accessible by rail, appear, and views of Lynmouth, first eulogized by Southey, St Mawgan-in-Pydar, near Newquay and Land's End were surely the result of holidays in Devon and Cornwall. The subject-matter throughout embodies the visual repertory of both guidebook and postcard: waterfall and windmill, sunset and stormy sea, rocky cliffhead and meandering river. And always, interspersed, nature study in the form of birds and sprays of flowers.

Compilations of this kind are quintessential expressions of the spread of literacy after the Education Act of 1870. The boom that followed in the production of new magazines and newspapers to feed this mass market was unprecedented. It was the era of the monthly illustrated magazine with its serialized novel. For the class of society to which Lawrence belonged such publications would have been the first initial contact with any form of graphic art and with this we can neatly place *The Seasons* in context. The composition of these pages with their picturesque topographical views, vignettes and contrived alphabets come directly out of a tradition of page layout combining text and illustration, established by Herbert Ingram in the *Illustrated London News* during the 1840s and '50s. John Gilbert was the head of a team of artists who created this style where the Victorian reader would find the content of the text expressed in the steel engravings. In an early issue of the magazine some rural scenes by Birket Foster, clearly a great influence on Lawrence, are accompanied by an exposition of these principles which read almost like a guide to those for *The Seasons*:

> Each bears the aspect of the month - a sort of pictured climatology, with the natural appearances of the season, and the monthly phases of the farmer's life. Thus, in January, the ground and roofs are thickly mantled with snow, the effect of which, against the black wintry sky, and the bare bough trees, is very telling; the scene is a farmyard, where the feeding of poultry, pigs and cattle, seems to break the sleep and silence of the season; the contrast of the still and busy life is excellent. The tail-piece is a shepherd carrying one of his flock in a snowstorm. The business of February is ploughing and sowing; the rooks are building, and all nature is just astir . . .

Lawrence's book is exactly like this, although he generally avoids figures and animals because they quickly reveal the limits of his capabilities. Lettering and landscape are his forte, although the charm of the book resides to a great extent in its amateur naivety. I have no doubt that a great many of the illustrations are directly lifted or reworked from contemporary magazines, nearly all of which featured seasonal lyrics and vignettes, but that in the end is not the point. It is the modesty, domesticity and the unquestioned sense of duty and values in this book that, a century later, most appeal to us. Doggerel the verse may often be but how evocative of the ethos of a period and of the man who was moved to compile this book.

SPRING.

While the earth remaineth, seed-time and harvest, and cold and heat, and summer and winter, and day and night shall not cease.

Genesis, VIII 22.

SUMMER.

AUTUMN.

All thy works shall give thanks unto thee, O Lord; and thy saints shall bless thee.

Psalm 145. 10. R.V.

WINTER.

L.G.L.

The Poems are by

M. Howitt,   M. R. Jarvis,   H. W. Longfellow,

J. Montgomery,   R. Southey,   W. Scott,

A. Tennyson,   R. Wilton,   W. Wordsworth,

Major W. A. H. Sigourney,

and many others.

The drawings are by

Louis Göttfried Lawrence.

1887 —— 1890.

St. Peter's,
Broadstairs.

"The
Seasons.

SPRING.

Ten thousand different
flowers
To Thee sweet offerings bear;
And cheerful birds, in shady
bowers,
Sing forth Thy tender care.

The fields on every side,
The trees on every hill,
The glorious sun,
the rolling tide,
Proclaim Thy wonders still.

But trees, and fields, and
skies,
Still praise a God unknown;
For gratitude and love can
rise
From living hearts alone.

These living hearts of ours,
Thy holy name would bless;
The blossoms of ten thousand
flowers
Would please the Saviour less.

While earth itself
decays,
Our souls can never die,
Oh, tune them all to
sing Thy praise
In better songs on high.

Blue-bells.

MAY-BLOSSOM.

Spring-evening.

The roseate hues of
early dawn,
The brightness of
the day,
The crimson of the
sunset sky,
How fast they fade away!
Oh, for the pearly gates
of heaven,
Oh, for the golden floor,
Oh, for the Sun of right-
eousness
That setteth nevermore!

Lo, the winter
is past,.....
The flowers appear on the earth;
The time of the singing of birds is come.

The Song of Songs.
Solomon, II. 11 & 12.

The winter time departeth;
The early flowers expand;
The blackbird and the turtle-dove
Are heard throughout the land.

Before us lies
the Spring-time—
Thank God, the time
of mirth—
When birds are singing
in the trees,
And flowers gem
all the earth.

M. Howitt.

"THE West wind has breathed
through the woodlands,
The sun lingereth lovingly there—
And the trees in a tremulous waking

Have clothed them in garments so fair
That we wander with hearts light as
childhood can know,
And feel that God's Heaven is round us below."

E. DAWSON.

"Thou blessest the

springing thereof."

Thou makest the outgoings of the
morning and evening to rejoice.
Thou visitest the earth, and waterest it;
the river of God is full of water: Thou providest them
corn, when Thou hast so prepared the earth.
Thou waterest her furrows abundantly;
Thou settlest the ridges thereof: Thou makest
it soft with showers; Thou blessest the
springing thereof. Thou crownest the year with
Thy goodness; and Thy paths drop fatness.
They drop upon the pastures of the
wilderness: and the hills are girded
with joy. The pastures are clothed with
flocks; the valleys also are covered over
with corn; they shout for joy,
they also sing."

Psalms, 65: 8-13. R.V.

What change is this
          that o'er the
               world appears?
It was but yesterday
     that all was tears
And sadness, and
          despair,
and wintry fears.

Now music of young
     voices fills the air;
   Grief is no more, and joy is everywhere;
     Colour and bloom where all was brown and bare!

Birds on the budding hedges sing and sway;
          The happy sunlight
                         fills the joyous day;
                    And skies are blue that first were dull
                                   and grey!

                    White clouds their fleeting
                              shadows lightly fling
                    O'er breezy upland
                              pastures; everything
                    Rejoices with the re-arisen Spring.

               Earth breaks the trammels of her
                              frost-bound prison,
               And after Winter's death finds life anew.

          Courage, faint heart! Awake! Thy Spring
                         is risen,
          Thou hast thy time of resurrection too.

                                   Helen Maud Waithman.

"Not worlds on worlds in phalanx deep,
   Need we to prove a God is here;
   The daisy, fresh from Nature's sleep,
Tells of His hand in lines as clear.
For who but He who arched the skies,
   And pours the day-spring's living flood,
   Wondrous alike in all He tries,
Could raise the daisy's crimson bud,
   And fling it, unrestrained and free,
      O'er hill and dale, and desert sod,
That man, where'er he walks, may see
      In every step the stamp of God!"

Good.

"Where thick thy primrose
         blossoms play,
Lovely and innocent as they,
Oer coppice, lawns,
         and dells,
In bands the rural
      children stray,
To pluck thy nectared
            bells."

Montgomery.

To the Cuckoo.

O blithe new-comer! I have heard,
  I hear thee and rejoice.
O Cuckoo! shall I call thee bird,
  Or but a wandering voice?

While I am lying on the grass,
  Thy twofold shout I hear,
From hill to hill it seems to pass,
  At once far off and near.

Though babbling only, to the vale,
  Of sunshine and of flowers,
Thou bringest unto me a tale
  Of visionary hours.

Thrice welcome; darling of the spring!
  Even yet thou art to me
No bird: but an invisible thing,
  A voice, a mystery.

The same whom in my school-boy days
  I listened to; that cry
Which made me look a thousand ways
  In bush, and tree, and sky.

To seek thee did I
          often rove
    Through woods and
              on the green;
  And thou wert still a hope,
          a love;
Still longed for, never seen.

      And I can listen to thee yet;
        Can lie upon
                  the plain
      And listen, till I do beget
          That golden time again.

O blessed bird!
      the earth we pace
Again appears
          to be
An unsubstantial
          faëry place;
  That is fit home
          for thee!

      W. Wordsworth.

"When Spring
unlocks the
flowers, to
paint the
laughing soil,
When Summer's
balmy showers refresh the
mower's toil,
When Winter binds in
frosty chains the
fallow and the flood —
In God the earth rejoiceth still,
and owns its
Maker good.

*   *   *   *

The flowers of Spring may wither,
  the hope of Summer fade,
The Autumn droop in Winter, the birds
          forsake the shade;
The wind be lulled,
          the sun and moon
          forget their old decree,
But we
      in nature's latest hour,
    O Lord!
  will cling
      to Thee."

Forget-me-Nots.

Weirdlaw Hill.

Weirdlaw Hill.

"The sun upon the Weirdlaw Hill,
   In Ettrick's vale, is sinking sweet;
The westland wind is hushed and still,
   The lake lies sleeping at my feet.
Yet not the landscape to mine eye
   Bears those sweet hues that once it bore;
Though Evening, with her richest dye,
   Flames o'er the hills of Ettrick shore."

WALTER SCOTT.

The Sky-lark

Oh, warn away the gloomy night! With music make the welkin ring; Bird of the dawn! on joyful wing, Soar through thine element of light, Till nought in heaven mine eye can see, Except the morning star and thee.

But speech of mine can ne'er reveal Secrets so freely told above; Yet is their burden joy and love, And all the bliss a bird can feel, Whose wing in heaven to earth is bound, Whose home and heart are on the ground.

Unlike the lark be thou, my friend! No downward cares thy thoughts engage; But, in thine house of pilgrimage, Though from the ground thy songs ascend, Still be their burden joy and love! Heaven is thy home, thy heart above.

Oh, welcome in the cheerful day! Through rosy clouds the shades retire; The sun hath touched thy plumes with fire, And girt thee with a golden ray; Now shape and voice are vanished quite, Nor eye nor ear can track their flight.

Might I translate thy strain, and give Words to thy notes in human tongue, The sweetest lay that e'er I sung, The lay that would the longest live, I should record upon this page, And sing thy song from age to age.

J. Montgomery.

Violets.

Arethusa.

"Arethusa arose
From her couch of snows
In the Acroceraunian mountains,—
From cloud and from crag
with many a jag,
Shepherding her bright fountains.
She leapt down the rocks
with her rainbow locks
Streaming among the
streams;

Her steps paved with green
        the downward ravine
Which slopes to the western gleams;
    And gliding and springing
            she went, ever singing;
In murmurs as soft as sleep;
    The earth seemed to love her,
        and heaven smiled above her,
            As she lingered towards the deep."

                                P. B. Shelley.

It is not always May.

The sun is bright, the air is clear,
　　The darting swallows soar
　　　　　　　　and sing,
And from the stately elms I hear
　　The blue-bird prophesying Spring.

So blue yon winding river flows,
　　It seems an outlet from the sky,
Where, waiting till the west wind blows,
　　The freighted clouds at anchor lie.

All things are new;— the buds, the leaves,
　　That gild the elm-tree's nodding crest,
And ev'n the nest beneath the eaves;—
　　There are no birds in last year's nest!

All things rejoice in youth and love,
　　The fulness of their first delight!
And learn from the soft heavens above
　　The melting tenderness of night.

Maiden, *
   that read'st
      this simple rhyme,
Enjoy thy youth,
         it will not stay;
   Enjoy the fragrance
            of thy prime,
      For O! it is not always May!

Enjoy the Spring of
            Love and Youth,
   To some good angel
            leave
               the rest;
   For time will teach thee
               soon the truth,

There are no birds in last year's nest!

                  H. W. Longfellow.

THE CHAFFINCH.

The Chaffinch

takes his summer rest
Among the fruit or forest trees,
Or in the hawthorn builds his nest,
Secure from pilfering enemies.

Aye welcome is his song, and when
Its early notes break on the ear,
A gladness fills the hearts of men,—
Their souls grow blithe with hopeful cheer;
For well they know it heralds Spring,
With buds and blossoms on her wing!
Come, then, O joyous bird, and be
The herald of a new-born glee,
The messenger of happy hours,
Of sunny skies and leafy bowers.

Hail, smiling morn!

Hail, smiling morn,
That tips the hills with gold,
Whose rosy fingers ope the gates of day,
Who the gay face of Nature doth unfold,
At whose bright presence darkness flies away.

"When from the opening chambers of the east
The morning springs, in thousand liveries drest,
The early larks their morning tribute pay,
And, in shrill notes, salute the blooming day.
Refreshèd fields with pearly dew do shine,
And tender blades therewith their tops incline.
Their painted leaves the unblown flowers expand,
And with their odorous breath perfume the land."

J. Thomson.

In the morning will I direct
my prayer unto Thee,
and will look up.

Psalm. 5: 3.

'If in the field I meet a smiling flower,
   Methinks it whispers,
            "God created me,
And I to Him devote my little hour,
   In lonely sweetness
            and humility."'

J. MONTGOMERY.

L.G.LAWRENCE.

SUMMER

Summer.

How beautiful is
summer when
the bee is on the wing,
And on the clustering hazel boughs the
linnets sit and sing;
Bright gladsome days of sunshine, the weary heart to cheer,
And chase the shades of sadness from the
anxious brow of care.

How beautiful the fields in their jewelled robe of green,
And the cool and shady lanes
where the sun is seldom seen;
Where at eve we love to wander and breathe the scented air,
Perfumed with sweetest odour
from the honeysuckle there.

A BREEZY MORNING.

How beautiful the billows that toss their foam on high,
And the placid lake reposing
beneath a cloudless sky;
The sparkling silver fountain in the cool delicious shade,
And the lowly streamlet murmuring
through the green and verdant glade.

How beautiful the happy homes
where England's sons
are reared,
But more happy still and hallowed
where God is loved and feared;
Where at morning and at evening
is heard the voice of prayer,
Commending every loved one to a
Father's tender care.

MARY EUGENIA.

It is summer! it is summer!
...how beautiful it looks!
There is sunshine on the old gray hills,
and sunshine on the brooks,
A singing-bird on every bough,
soft perfumes on the air,
A happy smile
on each young lip,
and gladness everywhere.

M. Howitt.

"Clear had the day been from the dawn,
All chequered was the sky,
Thin clouds like scarfs
of cobweb lawn
Veiled heaven's most
glorious eye.
The wind had no more
strength than this,
That leisurely
it blew,
To make one leaf
the next to kiss
That closely
by it grew."

M. Drayton.

In the Sunshine

"Live in the sunshine," the skylark
   Giving a voice   is singing,
      to the glad summer day;
Out of the azure his clear notes
        are ringing—
"Live in the sunshine, and sing
      while you may."

Clover and daisy-moons, high in
 Breathe   the meadows,
    the same secret of living aright,
 Lifting their bright heads afar
      from the shadows—
"Live in the sunshine and grow in the light."

So sings the brooklet, the hillside adorning, Flashing and sparkling with beauty aglow—
"Live in the sunshine and filled with the morning, Carry its brightness wherever you go!"

God of the sunshine, its Maker and Giver, Who to Thine own art a sun and a shield,
Teach us, we pray Thee, by song-bird and river,
      Help us to live as the flowers of the field.

Give us a heart to be trusting and cheerful,
   When in the shadows Thy love hath allowed:
And should our weak faith be downcast and fearful,
     Doubting Thy mercy when under the cloud—

Light of the wide world, arise for our healing,
   Scatter our gloom with the sunbeams
       of grace;
Shine on us, Lord, and Thy glory revealing,
   Make us to dwell in the light of Thy face!

MARY ROWLES JARVIS.

STAY near me—
do not take thy flight!
A little longer stay in sight!
Much converse do I find in thee,
Historian of my infancy!
Float near me; do not yet depart!
Dead times revive in thee:
Thou bring'st, gay creature as
thou art!
A solemn image to my heart,
My father's family!

Oh! pleasant, pleasant were the days,
The time, when, in our childish plays,
My sister Emmeline and I
Together chased the butterfly!
A very hunter did I rush
Upon the prey:—with leaps and springs
I followed on from brake to bush;
But she, God love her! feared to brush
The dust from off its wings.

W. Wordsworth.

There is an hour
in Summer's
busy day
When Nature seems to
pause, and over all
Comes a brief
sleep, hush'd with
the lullaby
Of myriad insects'
wings, and now
some small
bird's call.

The earth lies trembling
'neath the sun's fierce ray,
The reapers slumber in the
shade; and soon
Some little village church-bell, far away,
Slowly and dreamily strikes the
hour of noon.

Soft—in the hush of noontide, as we stand,
The waking world a dreamland's fantasy—
There comes a whisper from the far-off land,
Bringing us nearer to great Nature's
mystery.
'Twas here—'tis gone; the reaper
whets his scythe.:
We hear the talk of men,
the hum of bees—
The world's awake again, the
birds sing blythe;
Now bright the river gleams
between the trees!

G. C.

Reflections.

O the fancies that arise
When the streams reflect the skies,
And the image of the heavenly in the
earthly glory lies!

As the shadows darker grow
In the river's tranquil flow,
Thought grows deep and still, recalling memories of long ago.

But the evening closes fast,
Soon the sunset will be past,
And the onward rippling waters reach the open sea at last.

M. R.

THE QUILL

"Happy seabirds!
    how they hover
        O'er yon headland's
            breezy crest,
And their tender nestlings cover
    With warm wing and downy breast.

Happy seabirds! gliding, glancing,
        Through the livelong summer day,
Where the merry waves are dancing
        In the broad and sunny bay.

Lovely birds! with graceful motion
        Giving life to rock and sand,
Adding beauty to the ocean,
        Adding beauty to the strand.

How the eye delights to follow
        Where they circle o'er the deep,
Or with swiftness of the swallow
        O'er the glassy waters sweep."

Rev. R. Wilton. M.A.

" How dear to me the hour when daylight dies,
      And sunbeams melt along the silent sea;

For then sweet dreams of other days arise,
      And memory breathes her vesper sigh to thee. "

T. MOORE.

Near the Source.

The Brook.

I come from haunts
        of coot and hern,
    I make a sudden sally,
    And sparkle out
            among the fern,
    To bicker down
            a valley.

    By thirty hills I hurry down,
        Or slip between
                the ridges,
    By twenty thorps, a little town,
        And half a hundred bridges.

Till last by Philip's farm
                I flow
        To join the brimming river,
    For men may come
            and men may go,
        But I go on
                for ever.

Rustic Bridge.
Lynmouth.

I chatter over
        stony ways,
In little sharps and
                trebles,
    I bubble into eddying bays,
            I babble on the pebbles.

With many a curve my banks I fret
        By many a field and fallow,
            And many a fairy foreland set
            With willow-weed and mallow.

            I chatter, chatter, as I flow
            To join the
                    brimming river,
            For men may come
                    and men may go,
            But I go on
                    for ever.

I wind about, and in
                    and out,
    With here
            a blossom sailing,
And here and there
                a lusty trout,
    And here and there
                a grayling,

And here
        and there   a foamy flake
    Upon me,
            as I travel
    With many a silvery   waterbreak
        Above the golden
                        gravel,

    And draw
        them all along,   and flow
        To join the   brimming river,
        For men may come
                    and men may go,
        But I go on for ever.

I steal by lawns
        and grassy plots,
    I slide by hazel
            covers;
I move the sweet
        forget-me-nots
    That grow for
            happy lovers.

    I slip, I slide,
            I gloom, I glance,
        Among my
            skimming swallows;
        I make the nettled sunbeam dance
                Against my sandy shallows.

                I murmur under moon
                        and stars
            In brambly wildernesses;
                I linger by my shingly bars;
            I loiter round
                    my cresses;

Mouth of the Rivulet.

And out again I curve and flow
To join the brimming river,
For men may come and men may go,
But I go on for ever.

A. Tennyson.

As the flight of a river
    that flows to the sea,
My soul rushes ever in tumult to thee.
    A two-fold existence, I am where thou art,
        My heart in the distance beats close to thy heart;

Look up, I am near thee, I gaze on thy face,
    I see thee, I hear thee, I feel thine embrace."

LORD LYTTON.

L.G.LAWRENCE. 1800

SUNRISE

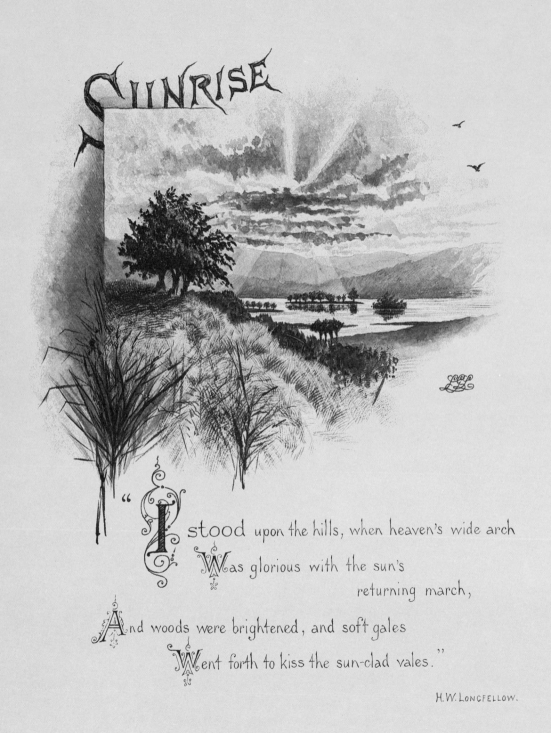

"I stood upon the hills, when heaven's wide arch
Was glorious with the sun's
returning march,
And woods were brightened, and soft gales
Went forth to kiss the sun-clad vales."

H. W. LONGFELLOW.

OH, happy day,
refuse to go!
Hang in the
heavens for
ever so!
For ever in mid-afternoon,
Ah, happy day of happy June!
Pour out thy sunshine on the h,
The piny wood with perfume fill,
And breathe across the
singing sea
Land-scented breezes,
that shall be
Sweet as the gardens
that they pass,
Where children tumble in
the grass!

Ah, happy day, refuse to go!
Hang in the heavens
for ever so!
And long not for thy blushing rest
In the soft-bosom of the west;
But bid gray evening get her back
With all the stars upon her track!
Forget the dark, forget the dew,
The mystery of the midnight blue,
And only spread thy wide warm wings
While summer her enchantment flings!

H. P. SPOFFORD.

CARISBROOKE CASTLE.

If thou art worn and hard beset With sorrows, that thou wouldst forget,
If thou wouldst read a lesson, that will keep Thy heart from fainting
and thy soul from sleep,
Go to the woods and hills!—No tears
Dim the sweet look that Nature wears.   H. W. LONGFELLOW.

Christ is all.

"Jesus, Refuge of my soul,
 Let me to Thy bosom fly,
While the raging waters roll;
 While the tempest still is high!
Hide me, O my Saviour, hide,
 Till the storm of life be past;
Safe into the haven guide;
 Oh receive my soul at last.

Other refuge have I none,
 Hangs my helpless soul on Thee!
Leave, ah! leave me not alone,
 Still support and comfort me!
All my trust on Thee is stayed;
 All my help from Thee I bring;
Cover my defenceless head
 With the shadow of Thy wing."

C. Wesley.

" He maketh the storm a calm,
so that the waves thereof are still.

Then are they glad because they be quiet;
so He bringeth them unto their
desired haven."

Psalm 107: 29 & 30.

Away to the woods.

Away to the woods, away;
All nature is smiling,
　　Our young hearts beguiling,
Oh, we will be happy to-day.
Away, away, away, away,
　　Away to the woods, away.

As free as the air are we;
　　Then rally, then rally,
　　From hill-top and valley,
And join in our innocent glee.

We all of us love the school;
　　And 'tis in well-doing
　　We're pleasure pursuing,
For truth is our guide and our rule.

Success to the school we love,
　　It sweetens employment
　　With harmless enjoyment,
And trains for the kingdom above.
Away, away, away, away,
　　Away to the woods, away.

Rev. A. A. Graley.

"In ripening Summer,
        the full laden vales
Give prospect of employment for
    the flails;
Each breath of wind the bearded
                groves makes bend,
Which seems the fatal sickle
                to portend."

J. Thomson.

"Lift up your eyes,
    and look on
        the fields,

That they are white
    already unto harvest."

S. John, 4: 35. R.V.

Daylight and Moonlight.

In broad daylight, and at noon
   Yesterday I saw the moon
Sailing high, but faint and white,
   As a schoolboy's paper kite.

In broad daylight yesterday,
   I read a Poet's mystic lay;
And it seemed to me at most
   As a phantom, or a ghost.

But at length the feverish day
   Like a passion died away,
And the night, serene and still,
   Fell on village, vale, and hill.

Then the moon, in all her pride,
   Like a spirit glorified,
Filled and overflowed the night
   With revelations of her light.

And the Poet's song again
   Passed like music through
      my brain;
Night interpreted to me
   All its grace and mystery.

H. W. Longfellow.

When the
last sunshine of
expiring day
In summer's twilight weeps itself
Who hath not felt   away,
the softness of the hour
Sink on the heart,
as dew along the flower?"

Lord Byron.

THE POND. BONCHURCH.

Morning.

Day had awakened all things that be,
The lark and the thrush and
the swallow free;
And the milkmaid's song and the mower's scythe,
And the matin-bell and the mountain bee:
Fireflies were quenched on the dewy corn,
Glow-worms went out on the river's brim,
Like lamps which a student forgets to trim,
The beetle forgot to wind his horn, The crickets were still in the meadow and hill:
Like a flock of rooks at a farmer's gun Night's dreams and
Fled from the brains   terrors, everyone,
which are their prey, From the lamp's death
to the morning ray.

SHELLEY.

" Hark! the lark at
heaven's gate sings."
SHAKSPEARE

The Spirit of Poetry.

TRERIEFE AVENUE, PENZANCE.

Lynmouth.
Cascade at the Water's Meet.

THERE is a quiet spirit in these woods,
That dwells where'er the gentle south wind blows;
Where, underneath the white-thorn, in the glade,
The wild-flowers bloom, or, kissing the soft air,
The leaves above their sunny palms outspread.
With what a tender and impassioned voice
It fills the nice and delicate ear of thought,

When the fast-ushering star of Morning comes
O'er-riding the grey hills with golden scarf;
Or when the cowled and dusky-sandaled Eve,
In mourning weeds, from out the western gate,
Departs with silent pace! That spirit moves
In the green valley, where the silver brook,
From its full laver, pours the white cascade;
And, babbling low amid the tangled woods,
Slips down through moss-grown stones with endless laughter.
And frequent, on the everlasting hills,
Its feet go forth, when it doth wrap itself
In all the dark embroidery of the storm,
And shouts the stern, strong wind. And here, amid
The silent majesty of these deep woods,
Its presence shall uplift thy thoughts from earth,
As to the sunshine and the pure, bright air
Their tops the green trees lift. Hence gifted bards
Have ever loved the calm and quiet shades.
For them there was an eloquent voice in all
The sylvan pomp of woods, the golden sun,
The flowers, the leaves, the river on its way,
Blue skies, and silver clouds, and gentle winds,—
The swelling upland, where the sidelong sun
Aslant the wooded slope, at evening, goes,—
Groves, through whose broken roof the sky looks in,
Mountain, and shattered cliff, and sunny vale,
The distant lake, fountains, and mighty trees,
In many a lazy syllable, repeating
Their old poetic legends to the wind.

And this is the sweet spirit, that doth fill
The world; and, in these wayward days of youth,
My busy fancy oft embodies it,
As a bright image of the light and beauty
That dwell in nature,—of the heavenly forms
We worship in our dreams, and the soft hues
That stain the wild bird's wing, and flush the clouds
When the sun sets. Within her eye
The heaven of April, with its changing light,
And when it wears the blue of May, is hung,
And on her lip the rich, red rose. Her hair Is like the summer tresses of the trees,
When twilight makes them brown, and on her cheek
Blushes the richness of an autumn sky,
With ever-shifting beauty. Then her breath, It is so like the gentle air of Spring,
As, from the morning's dewy flowers, it comes
Full of their fragrance, that it is a joy
To have it round us,—and her silver voice Is the rich music of a summer bird,
Heard in the still night,
with its passionate cadence.

H. W. LONGFELLOW.

Ecclesbourne Glen, Hastings.

"Pleasant it was, when woods were green,
    And winds were soft and low,
To lie amid some sylvan scene,
    Where, the long drooping boughs between,
Shadows dark and sunlight sheen
        Alternate come and go;
Or, where the denser grove receives
        No sunlight from above,
But the dark foliage interweaves
        In one unbroken roof of leaves,
Underneath whose sloping eaves
        The shadows hardly move."

H. W. LONGFELLOW.

CARNANTON WOODS. S. MAWGAN.

O my
garden full of singing
From the birds that house therein,
Sweet notes down the sweet day
ringing
Till the nightingales
begin!

THINK! the shadow on
the dial
For the nature most undone,
Marks the passing of
the trial,
Proves the presence of the sun!

Mrs. Browning.

AUTUMN.

With what a glory comes
and goes the year!
The buds of spring,
those beautiful harbingers
Of sunny skies and cloudless times, enjoy
Life's newness, and earth's
garniture spread out;
And when the silver habit of the clouds
Comes down upon the autumn sun,
and with
A sober gladness the old year
takes up
His bright inheritance of golden fruits,
A pomp and pageant fill the
splendid scene.
There is a beautiful spirit breathing now
Its mellow richness on the
clustered trees,
And, from a beaker full of richest
dyes,
Pouring new
glory on
the autumn woods,
And dipping in warm light
the pillard clouds.
Morn on the mountain, like
a summer bird,
Lifts up her purple wing,
and in the vales

The gentle wind,
a sweet and
passionate wooer,
Kisses the
blushing leaf,
and stirs up life
Within the solemn woods
of ash deep-crimsoned,
And silver beech, and maple yellow-leaved,
Where autumn, like a faint old man, sits down
By the wayside a-weary. Through the trees
The golden robin moves. The purple finch,
That on wild cherry and red cedar feeds,
A winter bird, comes with its plaintive
whistle,
And pecks by the witch-hazel,
whilst aloud
From cottage roofs the
warbling blue-bird sings,
And merrily, with oft-repeated stroke,
Sounds from the threshing-floor the busy flail.

O what a glory doth this world put on
For him who, with a fervent heart, goes forth
Under the bright and glorious sky, and looks
On duties well performed, and days well spent!

For him the wind, ay, and the yellow leaves,
Shall have a voice, and give him
eloquent teachings.
He shall so hear the solemn hymn,
that Death
Has lifted up for all, that he shall go
To his long resting-place
without a tear.

H. W. LONGFELLOW.

Brightly shines the
    Sabbath day,
Calm and peaceful is the morn,
As the farmer wends his way
    Through the sheaves
        of golden corn.

Six days fall the ripened ears,
    Fields are crowned with sheaf
            on sheaf;
Then the Sabbath day
    For the labourer's appears
            relief.

    See the sheaves in goodly rows
        Glistening in the autumn sun;
    Oh, what thanks the farmer owes For the great things God has done.
    Happy he who stays his hand, Both in soul and substance blest,
        And obeys the Lord's command Even in harvest time to rest.

Happy he who gladly leaves Liberal gleanings to the poor,
        Nor sweeps all his golden sheaves
                Into his own threshing floor.
        From the corners of his field*
                He will not clean riddance make
        But to God a portion yield
                For the poor and stranger's sake.

Every sheaf poor widows glean
From a Christian's fruitful ground
Shall in heavenly barns
  be seen,
And to his account abound.
God remembers those above
Who His Word remember here,
Who His Sabbaths keep and love,
  And His poor relieve and cheer.

Blest their name and home shall be,
  Blest their basket and their store,
  God's salvation they shall see,
    Blest in heaven for evermore!

R. WILTON. M.A.

*"When ye reap the harvest of your land, thou shalt not
make clean riddance of the corners of thy field when
thou reapest, neither shalt thou gather any gleaning
of thy harvest: thou shalt leave them unto the
poor, and to the stranger: I am the Lord your **God.**"

"When ye reap the harvest of your land, thou **shalt**
not wholly reap the corners of thy field,
neither shalt thou gather the gleanings
of thy harvest."

LEVITICUS, XXIII. 22. and XIX. 9.

"Observe
  How soon the golden field
    abounds with sheaves;
How soon the
    oat and bearded barley fall,
In frequent lines before the keen-edged scythe;
  The clattering team then comes, the
        swarthy hind
Down leaps and doffs his frock alert and plies
        The shining fork."

HURDIS.

Bonchurch.
The old church.

"Safe, safe upon the
ever-shining shore,
Sin, pain, and death,
and sorrow, all are o'er;
Happy now and
evermore,
Washed in the blood
of the Lamb."

God's-Acre.

God's-Acre.

I like that ancient Saxon phrase,
                        which calls
        The burial-ground God's-Acre! It is just;
    It consecrates each grave within its walls,
        And breathes a benison o'er the sleeping dust.

God's-Acre! Yes, that blessed name imparts
        Comfort to those who in the grave have sown
The seed, that they had garnered in their hearts,
        Their bread of life, alas! no more their own.

Into its furrows shall we all be cast,
        In the sure faith that we shall rise again
At the great harvest, when the archangel's blast
        Shall winnow, like a fan, the chaff and grain.

Then shall the good stand in immortal bloom,
        In the fair gardens of that second birth;
And each bright blossom mingle its perfume
        With that of flowers, which never bloomed on earth.

With thy rude ploughshare, Death, turn up the sod,
        And spread the furrow for the seed we sow;
This is the field and Acre of our God,
        This is the place where human harvests grow.

H. W. Longfellow.

"Abide with us: for it is toward evening, and the day is now far spent. And He went in to abide with them."

S. Luke, 24. 29.

Abide with me, fast falls the eventide:
The darkness thickens: Lord, with me abide.
When other helpers fail, and comforts flee, Help of the helpless, O abide with me.

Swift to its close ebbs out life's little day; Earth's joys grow dim, its glories pass away;
Change and decay in all around I see: O Thou who changest not, abide with me.

Not a brief glance I beg, a passing word, But as Thou dwell'st with
Thy disciples, Lord:
Familiar, condescending, patient, free, Come not to sojourn, but abide with me.

Come not in terrors, as the Kings of kings, But kind and good, with healing in
Thy wings;
Tears for all woes, a heart for every plea; Come, Friend of sinners, thus abide with me.

I need Thy presence every passing hour;
What but Thy grace can foil the tempter's power?
Who like Thyself my guide and stay can be? Through cloud and sunshine,
O abide with me.

I fear no foe, with Thee at hand to bless, Ills have no weight, and tears no bitterness.
Where is Death's sting? where, Grave, thy victory? I triumph still, if Thou abide with me.

Reveal Thyself before my closing eyes, Shine through the gloom, and
point me to the skies:
Heaven's morning breaks, and earth's vain shadows flee:
In life, in death, O Lord, abide with me.

H. F. Lyte.

" Until the day break,

and the shadows
flee away. "

Solomon's Song. 2:17.

Land's End

"Ye were as sheep going astray;
but are now returned."

I. Peter, II 25.

I was a wandering sheep,
I did not love the fold;
I did not love my Shepherd's
voice,
I would not be controlled.
I was a wayward child,
I did not love my home,
I did not love my Father's voice,
I loved afar to roam.

Jesus my Shepherd is;
'Twas He that loved my soul,
'Twas He that washed me
in His blood,
'Twas He that made me whole.
'Twas He that sought the lost,
That found the wandering sheep;
'Twas He that brought me to the fold,
'Tis He that still doth keep.

The Shepherd sought His
sheep,
The Father sought His
child;
They followed me o'er vale and hill,
O'er deserts waste and wild.
They found me nigh to death,
Famished, and faint, and lone;
They bound me with the bands
of love,
They saved the wandering one.

I was a wandering sheep,
I would not be controlled,
But now I love my Shepherd's
voice,
I love, I love the fold!
I was a wayward child,
I once preferred to roam;
But now I love
my Father's voice,
I love,
I love His home!

H. BONAR.

Linger, O gentle Time!
Linger, O radiant grace of bright To-day!
Let not the hours' chime
Call thee away,
But linger near me still with fond delay.

Linger, for thou art mine!
What dearer treasures can the future hold?
What sweeter flowers than thine
Can she unfold?
What secrets tell my heart thou hast not told.

Oh linger in thy flight!
For shadows gather round, and should we part
A dreary, starless night
May fill my heart —
Then pause and linger yet, ere thou depart.

Adelaide Procter.

"All my springs
are in Thee."

Psalm 87: 7.

"It is from hills that rivers wind,
Enriching all their course —
And so, with happy lives — we find
They have a lofty source."

EDEN HOOPER.

"As down in the sunless retreats of the ocean,
   Sweet flowers are springing no
                           mortal can see,
So, deep in my soul the still prayer of devotion,
   Unheard by the world,
                     rises silent to Thee,
   My God! silent to Thee—
         Pure, warm, silent to Thee."

THOMAS MOORE.

DOVER CASTLE.

The Lord is my rock, and my fortress, and my deliverer, even mine; the God of my rock, in him will I trust; my shield, and the horn of my salvation, my high tower, and my refuge.

2. SAM. XXII. 2, 3. R.V.

To him that overcometh will I grant to sit with me in my throne, even as I also overcame, and am set down with my Father in his throne.

REV. III, 21.

I

Thou art,
O God,
the life and light

Of all this wondrous world we see;
Its glow by day, its smile by night, Are but reflections caught from Thee.
Where'er we turn, thy glories shine,
And all things fair and bright are Thine!

III When Night, with wings of starry gloom,
O'ershadows all the earth and skies,
Like some dark, beauteous bird, whose plume
Is sparkling with unnumber'd eyes—
That sacred gloom, those fires divine,
So grand, so countless, Lord! are Thine.

II When Day, with farewell beam, delays
Among the op'ning clouds of Even,
And we can almost think we gaze
Through golden vistas into Heaven—
Those hues that make the Sun's decline
So soft, so radiant, Lord! are Thine.

IV When youthful Spring around us breathes,
Thy Spirit warms her fragrant sigh;
And ev'ry flower the
Summer wreathes
Is born beneath that
kindling eye.
Where'er we turn,
thy glories shine,
And all things
fair and bright
are Thine!

T. Moore.

Grasmere.

Go in peace!
  The sun is sinking—
  Weary breezes die away;
Lo, the threads of sunlight linking
  Lengthen thro' the woodlands grey!

Tiny rays of golden, peeping
    Through the tangles
        of the green,
Where the mossy brook is creeping,
    While the pathway winds between;

Like the glimpses of a gladness
    Such as mortals seldom know,
        And an earnest, 'mid our sadness,
            Of a joy that will not go.

Often, thus when Day is ending,
    And the sunlight falls to rest,
While the sleepy willows bending
    Kiss the mere's unruffled breast,

Doth the brightness of the gleaming
    Find its way to shady nooks,
        Which the noontide's warmest beaming
            Could not pierce
                with sunny looks.

A. L. SALMON.

Mine be a cot beside a hill,
A beehive's hum shall soothe my ear;
A willowy brook that turns a mill
With many a fall, shall linger near.

The swallow oft, beneath my thatch,
Shall twitter from
        her clay-built nest;
Oft shall the pilgrim
        lift the latch
And share my meal,
        a welcome guest.

Around my ivied porch shall spring
    Each fragrant flower
        that drinks the dew,
And Lucy, at her wheel,
        shall sing
    In russet gown and apron blue.

The village church among the trees,
    Where first our marriage vows were given,
With merry peals shall swell the breeze,
    And point with
        taper spire to heaven.

Rogers.

Twilight.

THE twilight is sad
　　　　and cloudy,
　　The wind blows wild
　　　　and free,
　　And like the wings of
　　　　sea-birds
　　Flash the white caps of
　　　　the sea.

But in the fisherman's cottage
　　There shines a ruddier light,
And a little face at the window
　　Peers out into the night.

Close, close it is pressed to
　　　　the window,
　　As if those childish eyes
Were looking into the darkness,
　　To see some form arise.

And a woman's waving
　　　　shadow
　　Is passing
　　　　to and fro,
　　Now rising to
　　　　the ceiling,
　　Now bowing and
　　　　bending low.

What tale do the roaring ocean,
　　And the night-wind, bleak and wild,
As they beat at the crazy casement,
　　Tell to that little child?

And why do the roaring ocean,
　　And the night-wind, wild and bleak,
As they beat at the heart
　　　　of the mother,
　　Drive the colour from her cheek?

H. W. Longfellow.

"The wind blows wild and free."

Old London Road, Hastings

"This is the day of toil
Beneath earth's sultry noon,
This is the day of service true,
But resting cometh soon."

H. BONAR.

The morning time is fresh and fair,
With scent of flowers in the air;
But soon the morning light
is past,
Or overcast.

The evening is the time of peace,
When work is done and
troubles cease,
And sunset lights our
quiet way
At end of day.

E. NESBIT.

UNDER a spreading
                chestnut-tree
The village smithy stands;
The smith, a mighty man is he,
    With large and sinewy hands;
And the muscles of
            his brawny arms
Are strong as iron bands.

His hair is crisp, and black, and long,
        His face is like the tan;
            His brow is wet
                with honest sweat,
    He earns whate'er he can,
He looks the whole world in the face,
        For he owes
                not any man.

Week in, week out, from morn till night,
    You can hear his bellows blow;
You can hear him swing his heavy sledge,
    With measured beat and slow,
    Like a sexton ringing the village bell,
        When the evening sun is low.

And children coming home
                    from school
    Look in at the open door;
They love to see the flaming forge,
    And hear the bellows roar,
And catch the burning
                    sparks that fly
    Like chaff from a
                    threshing-floor.

He goes on Sunday to the church,
    And sits among his boys;
    He hears the parson pray and preach,
        He hears his daughter's voice,
Singing in the village choir,
        And it makes his
                    heart rejoice.

It sounds to him like her
                    mother's voice,
    Singing in Paradise!
He needs must think of her
                    once more,
How in the grave she lies;
    And with his hard, rough
                    hand he wipes
    A tear out of his eyes.

TOILING—REJOICING—
    sorrowing,
Onward through
        life he goes;
Each morning sees some task begun,
Each evening sees it close;
Something attempted, something done,
Has earned a night's repose.

Thanks, thanks to thee,
        my worthy friend,
For the lesson thou hast taught!
Thus at the flaming
            forge of life
Our fortunes must be wrought;
Thus on its sounding
            anvil shaped
Each burning
    deed and
        thought.

H. W. LONGFELLOW.

WINTER.

When Winter winds are piercing chill,

And through the hawthorn blows the gale, With solemn feet I tread the hill
That overbrows the lonely vale.

O'er the bare upland, and away Through the long reach of desert woods,
The embracing sunbeams chastely play,
And gladden these deep solitudes.

There, twisted round the barren oak, The summer vine in beauty clung,
And summer winds the stillness broke, The crystal icicle is hung.

There, from their frozen urns, mute springs Pour out the river's gradual tide,
Shrilly the skater's iron rings,
And voices fill the woodland side.

Alas! how changed from the fair scene, When birds sang out their mellow lay,
And winds were soft, and woods were green,
And the song ceased not with the day.

But still wild music is abroad, Pale, desert woods! within your crowd;
And gathering winds, in hoarse accord,
Amid the vocal reeds pipe loud.

Chill airs and wintry winds! my ear Has grown familiar with your song;
I hear it in the opening year,—
I listen, and it
cheers me long.

H. W. LONGFELLOW.

"The embracing sunbeams
chastely play."

WINTER.

Though now no more the
                musing ear
        Delights to listen to the breeze,
That lingers   o'er the greenwood shade,
        I love thee, Winter, well.
The green moss shines with icy glare
        The long grass bends its
                spear-like form
And lovely is the
        silvery scene,
        When faint the sunbeams smile.

                                    R. Southey.

SNOW-FLAKES.

Out of the bosom of the Air, Out of the cloud-folds of her garments shaken,
Over the woodlands brown and bare, Over the harvest-fields forsaken,
        Silent, and soft, and slow Descends the snow.

Even as our cloudy fancies take Suddenly shape in some divine expression,
Even as the troubled heart doth make In the white countenance confession,
        The troubled sky reveals The grief it feels.

This is the poem of the Air, Slowly in silent syllables recorded;
        This is the secret of despair, Long in its cloudy bosom hoarded,
        Now whispered and revealed
                To wood and field.

                                    H. W. Longfellow.

How soft the music
of those village bells,
Falling at intervals upon the ear
In cadence sweet;
now dying all away,
Now pealing loud again, and
louder still.
. . . .
At noon,
Upon the southern side of the
slant hills,
And where the woods fence off
the northern blast,
The season smiles, resigning all its rage,
And has the warmth of May. The vault is blue
Without a cloud, and white without a speck

The dazzling splendour of the scene below.
Again the harmony comes o'er the vale;
And through the trees I view th' embattled tower,
Whence all the music. I again perceive
The soothing influence of the wafted strains,
And settle in soft musings as I tread
The walk, still verdant, under oak and elms.
The redbreast warbles still, but is content
With slender notes, and more than half
suppressed
Pleased with his solitude, and
flitting light
From spray to spray, where'er he
rest he shakes
From many a twig the
pendent drops of ice,
That tinkle in the withered leaves below.

THE CURTAIN OF THE DARK.

THE curtain of the dark
　　Is pierced by many a rent :
　　　Out of the star-wells, spark on spark
　　　Trickles through night's torn tent.

GRIEF is a tattered tent,
　　　Where through
　　　　God's light doth shine.
Who glances up at every rent
　　　Shall catch a ray divine.

LARCOM.

Lead, kindly Light,

amid the encircling gloom,
Lead Thou me on:
The night is dark, and I am far from home,
Lead Thou me on:
Keep Thou my feet; I do not ask to see
The distant scene;
one step enough for me.

I was not ever thus, nor prayed that Thou
Shouldst lead me on:
I loved to choose and see my path, but now
Lead Thou me on:
I loved the garish day, and, spite of fears,
Pride ruled my will;
remember not past years.

So long Thy power hath blest me, sure it still
Will lead me on
O'er moor and fen,
o'er crag and torrent, till
The night is gone,
And with the morn those angel faces smile,
Which I have loved long since,
and lost awhile.

J. H. NEWMAN.

My Father's at the Helm.

The curling waves with awful roar,

A gallant ship assailed,

And pallid fear's distracting power

O'er all on board prevailed;